Sienna - Fairy Coloring Book:
Grayscale Edition

First published October 2019
Published by Michelle Tracey
www.michelletraceyart.com

I.S.B.N: 978-0-9945155-8-2

Copyright © 2019 Michelle Tracey
All Rights Reserved.

No part of this book may be reproduced, stored in a retrieval system, or transmitted, in any form or by any means (electronic, mechanical, photocopying, recording or otherwise) without the prior written permission from the publisher.

Who is Sienna?

Sienna is a celestial fairy from the stars, guiding humans on their Earth journey, enhancing our connection with all. By shining a light on our path she works to raise our vibrations, illuminate our minds and activate our hearts to their true potential.

Sienna reminds us of the light within, how this connects us to nature and all her creatures, to Source, the Universe and all souls. Her message is one of hope and empowerment, encouraging all people of Earth to follow their own light, to shine bright like the unique star they are.

Who is the Deer?

Sienna's loving companion the deer is part of her soul family, sharing the same star markings as Sienna. Like humans, Sienna also cares for animals, nurturing their spirits and helping them find their way home. The beautiful deer shares with us messages of kindness, gentleness, acceptance and unconditional love.

Symbols

A powerful symbol is featured in each painting to infuse the artwork with high vibrational healing energies. The symbols include aspects of Reiki, Rune and Celtic impressions. Can you find them?

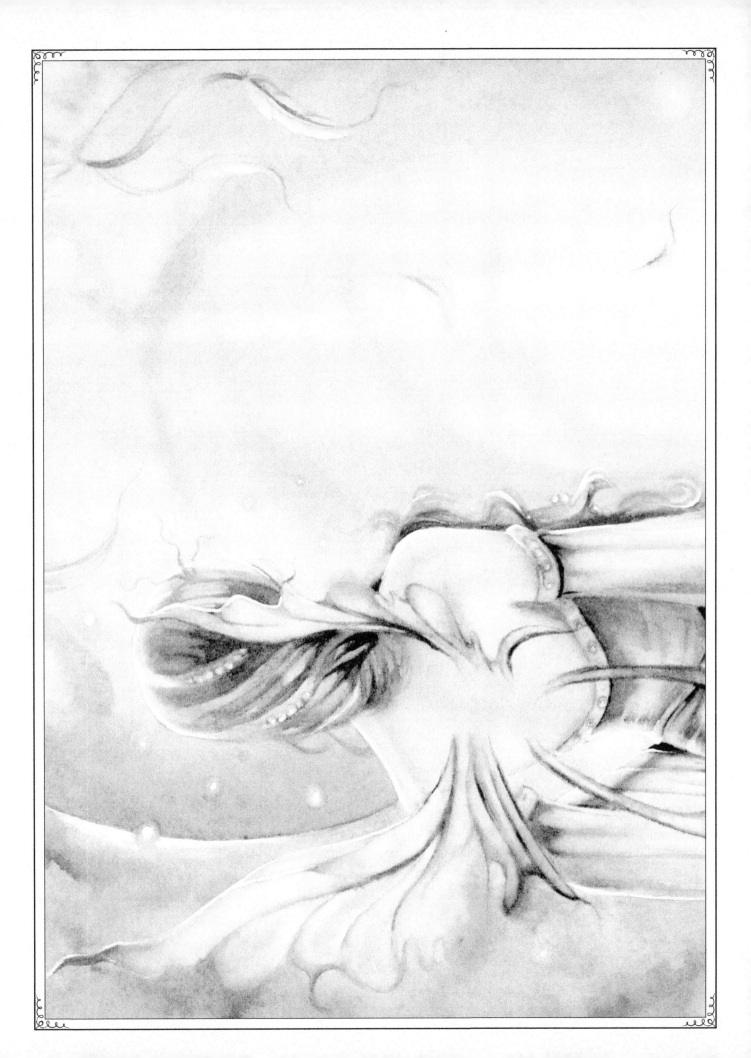

about the Artist

> *"My Mission is to INSPIRE the soul, to enrich lives through the connection of spiritual awareness by helping people connect with their spiritual selves."*
>
> *- Michelle Tracey*

Michelle Tracey is a spiritual fantasy artist and coloring book author living on the Central Coast of NSW, Australia. It is Michelle's Mission inspire the soul, to enrich lives through the connection of spiritual awareness. To ignite and raise this awareness, Michelle delivers inspiring messages through her beautiful fantasy artwork. Each creation is designed to convey emotion and awaken contemplation, whilst restoring hope, divine guidance and insight.

Michelle understands the spiritual disconnect that can be experienced when we are caught up in the physical world of day to day life. It is her vision to inspire the World, to shine light and magic into hearts and souls.

JOIN MICHELLE'S ART & COLORING TRIBE AND CHECK OUT **MORE** Coloring Books!

COLORING BOOKS/PAGES
Purchase Coloring Pages and Books (Instant Downloads)
www.michelletraceyart.com

COLORING BOOKS/PAGES
Purchase Coloring Pages and Books (Instant Downloads)
www.etsy.com/shop/MichelleTraceyArt

SUBSCRIBE
Coloring Tutorials & Behind the Scenes Footage
www.youtube.com/c/MichelleTraceyArt

FAN PHOTOS
Share Your Finished Coloring Pages on Michelle's Page
www.facebook.com/michelletraceyart

YOU'RE INVITED TO JOIN A GROUP
Michelle Tracey's Colouring Tribe
www.facebook.com/groups/michelletraceyscolouringtribe

NEWSLETTER SIGN UP
FREEBIES! Giveaways & News on Art & Coloring Books
www.eepurl.com/bUTzo1

INSTAGRAM
Follow Michelle on Instagram
www.instagram.com/michelletraceyart

PINTEREST
Follow Michelle on Pinterest
www.pinterest.com/michelletraceyart

More Products Available
www.michelletraceyart.com

Made in the USA
Las Vegas, NV
10 April 2022